AF483697

This book belongs to:

____

WRITTEN BY JULIA BERDICHEVSKAYA   ILLUSTRATED BY NATALIIA MATIUSHKO

THE HAPPY FOOD GARDEN PARTY

Tony and Sonya the curious and health–conscious friends, were back for another exciting adventure. After their wonderful journey through the world of HEALTHY EATING, they decided it was time to bring the magic of food to their own backyard.

One sunny day, Tony and Sonya gathered their friends and family for a special event—a HAPPY FOOD GARDEN PARTY!

They set up colorful tables and chairs surrounded by blooming flowers and green plants. The air was filled with LAUGHTER and the aroma of DELICIOUS, HEALTHY TREATS.

SMOOTHIE

Their first stop at the garden party was the smoothie station. Tony and Sonya had collected a variety of fresh fruits and vegetables, such as STRAWBERRIES, BANANAS, SPINACH, and CARROTS.

They blended them all together to create TASTY and NUTRITIOUS SMOOTHIES. Their friends took turns picking their favorite ingredients and enjoyed sipping on their custom-made drinks.

Next, they had a vegetable painting station. Tony and Sonya had set up easels and provided paintbrushes and colorful vegetable paints made from BEETS, TURMERIC, and other NATURAL INGREDIENTS.

The children used their artistic skills to paint beautiful pictures using the vibrant vegetable colors. They giggled as they painted with CARROTS, CELERY, and BROCCOLI, turning healthy veggies into works of art.

As the party continued, they moved to the garden to learn about growing their own food. Tony and Sonya showed their friends how to plant seeds in pots and nurture them with sunlight and water. They explained that growing their own fruits and vegetables was not only fun but also a great way to enjoy FRESH, ORGANIC PRODUCE.

The highlight of the party was the healthy snack buffet. Tony and Sonya had prepared a feast of colorful SALADS, crunchy VEGETABLE STICKS with dip, and FRUIT SKEWERS.

Their friends filled their plates with a rainbow of nutritious foods, savoring each bite. They discovered that healthy snacks could be just as TASTY and EXCITING as sugary treats.

HONEY

Before the day came to an end, Tony and Sonya shared their secret recipe for A SPECIAL DESSERT — HEALTHY, HOMEMADE POPSICLES. They mixed pureed fruits like MANGO, BLUEBERRIES, and WATERMELON with a touch of natural HONEY, poured the mixture into molds, and froze them. The children happily licked their fruity popsicles, feeling refreshed and satisfied.

As the sun began to set, the children bid farewell to the HAPPY FOOD GARDEN PARTY, carrying with them the joy of delicious and healthy eating. Tony and Sonya knew that their adventure had inspired everyone to make healthy choices and enjoy the magic of food.

And so, my little friends, let the HAPPY FOOD GARDEN PARTY be a reminder that healthy eating is not only good for your body but also a wonderful way to celebrate with friends and family. Grow your own food, explore new flavors, and let the magic of food bring happiness to your lives.

THE HAPPY FOOD
GARDEN PARTY
COLORING PAGES

SMOOTHIE TIME!